GRIEF LIKE A

by

Josie Davies

Typeset and Published by
The National Poetry Foundation
(Registered Charity No 283032)
27 Mill Road
Fareham
Hants PO16 0TH
(Tel/Fax 01329 822218)

Printed by
Consort Print Services
Consort Court, High Street
Fareham, Hants PO16 7AL
(Tel 01329 822530)

.

Sponsored by Rosemary Arthur

Cover photograph by Celia Rambaut

Edited by Johnathon Clifford

Poems previously published by *Ammonite, Chester Poets, Envoi, Folio International, Pause, Periaktos, Poetry Nottingham, Salopeot, Spokes, Success, Summit* and *Weyfarers.*

ISBN 1 900726 15 7

CONTENTS

To my dear Husband, Dai;
to Margaret Munro Gibson and to all those friends
who gave me support and encouragement
during his long illness . . .

And to Teresa Randle,
who opened my eyes and ears to poetry
and who has been such a patient listener.

GRIEVING WILD

Grief, like a tiger
hungry in the night
striping silence,
whets his appetite on dreams
and captures sleep.

Or, like a snake
inching dark in sunlight,
grows fat on thoughts
of golden afternoons . . .
and swallows them whole.

Flashing brilliance,
exotic birds high flying
lift the eye
but parrot-scream
fades colours fast

to dusk . . . and a jackal
howling hours lost.
From ancient waterhole
the elephants drink deep,
blot out the moon

and grief, like a tiger
hungry in the night,
kills sleep.

STROKE

1.

Morning arrived in hobnailed boots
thumping through dreams
leaving their imprint on the day.

Leather-stout, you stalked the sun
always deceived by superficial shine

but soles wear thin
and afternoon split open at the seams
taking you in to gaping dark.

When evening gentled by barefoot,
I found you slippered, soft
and almost whole again.

2.

That night,
sleep was left standing.
It was the train that wakened him -
screaming discord
through his brain,
swaying madly over points of pain . . .
the train.

And then the people came:
thin, grey figures
filing past the bed
as if in never ending
lines of dread.
He said:
They come for tickets.

Sleep was dead.

3.

Breakfast, a simple meal
of cereal and toast (not
over-brown, the crust removed)
was late.

Time was not the catalyst
for what had gone before,
but hate released by chance
and human frailty.
And on that day,
innocuous to folk outside,
we played at war.

Commands to unknown soldiers
ricocheted off walls;
and those less fortunate were lined
along the hallway of his mind
facing the barrel
of his walking stick
held shoulder high.

Ranked Private, I preceded him
from room to room
in search of spies,
to prise out possibilities
and probe each threat
in his fragmented sight.
Then, in the garden, summer-hot
we shot deserters
dark behind the potting shed.

Inside his head
the battle raged until he fell
in no man's land again -
that pitted moonscape of the soul
where reason lies
abandoned on barbed wire.

Out of the mire, inch by inch
along a well-worn track and straight,
we made it back.
But breakfast - just a simple meal
of cereal and toast,
was late.

4.

Today, you lie
imprisoned in a Parker Knoll
grasping illusion out of air.
Restive, you circle wasted limbs . . .
pedalling despair.

Footnote: Dai passed away in December 1995

SIMILE IN A BUS SHELTER

Small boy, restless as the wind,
mongol eyes aslant
in a face with nothing much to say.

Rolling around the metal cage
quite unaware,
he only stared:

his fears
of things not understood -
a murky pond
replenished by the day.

He stood there framed in space
where glass had given up brief tenancy,
a desperation in his fingers
crooked and pleading, 'Come'.

His face, his fingers lingered:
melodies elusive at the start,
returning . . .

FREAK SNOW

Suddenly,
sheep in the garden:
rotund, white, abundant creatures
huddled under trees
lolling indolently along the borders.

Quite unperturbed
by starlings
skittering down broad backs,
they stayed all day -
adipose, feeding on time,
heavy with fleecy folds
made crystalline
in Arctic wind.

By night,
warm air from Africa
reduced the flocks
to dripping skeletons
and in the morning, they were gone -

the only sign
of this strange birth and death . . .

(like tufts of wool caught
upon tiny hedgerow twigs)
droplets of water
glistening in the sun.

CUTTING EDGE - NORTHERN IRELAND 1994

Too late for apologies,
if only this or that . . .
It is midnight,
the most important kind
strap-hanging years
between it was and will be:
dark hour of Roman Candles
and of rocket bursts
exploding cloistered silence -
this curtained space
where I lie trapped
in probabilities.

Sound distorts
confuses time and place,
rattles like gunfire in my head
and resolutions fade
more quickly than a Christmas truce.
It is midnight -
and three more dead:

three fathers drinking celebration,
felled before the froth is blown -
and shivering by angry fires,
three mothers sobbing
over long cold desires.

A tall enough child
removes the fairy from the tree.
It is midnight -
and too late for apologies.

THE ROOF

Prologue.

She saw herself reflected in the house
hard pressed by age and circumstance.
She knew the signs of stress - a tile
gone missing here and there,
the downward curve, the sag.
"It cannot be denied"
the roofer said, "this flattening out
is putting pressure on the eaves,
which leaves me in no doubt -
no doubt at all
your purlins are the problem here.
A nasty bow you've got and that's no good.
We need some wood, a metal strip
and bolts, new felting, flashing . . ." on and on.
She wished the cause of her malaise
could be nailed down
and remedied with such aplomb.
She shivered and walked painfully indoors.

1. *Scaffolding.*

They came in rain to cage the day,
board off the sun
should it be brave enough
to fly an English sky in June.
April and May were Spanish-hot
then . . . not.

Bars rust thrust
bone upwards tower-tall,
traverse and lock;
joints tighten sinews
stretched too thin,
imprison house and all within
except for cats high-tailing it
on feline walkways custom made;
the world reduced inside a metal box
where she sits small and waits.

2. *Stripping.*

It was not a neat, methodical affair
as she had thought -
a careful easing off
or slick removal of a tired skin.
The end came in a thunderous cascade
of stubble, rubble
husk and chaff -
a rush of slough.

3. *Strengthening.*

The men had come
hung-over from the night before.

Not yet in working mode, the pair
stay van-side supping tea,
procrastinate. Timber trails late

9

(somewhere an order went astray)
and then from an uncomfortable peace
(all men, machines in place) -
the first reverberating strike
of steel on brick, on wood
on mind on head.
Electric drill and power saw
cut in and out
like some demented giant snore
in nightmare and delirium . . .

until the beams of fifty years
are reinforced, made sound
and buttressed, bolted firm.

Below, in order to confound
malicious gods,
she types a sonnet -
gentle counterpoint to war.

4. *Tiling.*

Today, if there is no delay
because of rain, or those
elastic tea breaks in the van,
the man and his accomplice
plan to start
the bonding of parts:

wounds to be wrapped and battened down,
new cladding grafted on
piece by interlocking piece -
a concrete carapace
lighter than before, less weight
for ageing body to support.

A firm cement between
the old and new is paramount,
straight ridged and true against the blue
(when there are gaps in cloud);
the chimneys standing proud
above lead flashing, valleys cut
and lined with fibreglass,
all verges undercloaked,
and modern gutters
to prevent her getting soaked.

Epilogue.

Last rites still have to be performed -
the debris of an almost lifetime
piling high is palleted
and stacked on roadside strip (the green
too sparse to qualify as grass)
awaiting transport to the tip.

She sleeps dream-free between two thoughts:
tomorrow they remove the bars,
give scars the space to heal . . .

MATINS FROM AN UPSTAIRS WINDOW

Lean trees, winter bare,
steeple the skyline
above a congregation of rooftops
huddled against sermons;

backyard pews, adrift with incense
from November fires.

Feathered gargoyles
watch from aluminium towers
but only weeds
brave the stony aisles . . .

and unbelieving cats.

Once-eager celebrants
no longer walk abroad to pray
but, locked in warm confessionals
with tea and toast,
worship before push-button gods.

A hungry dog howls requiem for hope

and sirens wail irreverently, Amen.

FOR WORSE . . .

In sprawling sleep's befuddled dreams
he still drinks deep.
The house sits silent, not one brick
dare tumble on his afternoon.

And in a corner, thinly pale,
a child marooned
with paper dolls to cut and dress,
refashion every day with brief desires
while in another space upstairs,
a woman weeps.

Through drunken dark
he staggers ragged
scarlet-loud
and mouthing black.

Small in a corner, thinly pale,
a child marooned
fighting the monsters on her back
while in another space somewhere
a woman wanting rainbows, weeps.

SLINGS AND ARROWS

The first stone was in no way
                    a surprise to him -
dark voices had rumbled the hills for days.

When light re-asserted itself,
                    the pebbles came
fine and smooth, tickling the man to laughter.

But it was a false spring. Rocks followed
pitted with flint, compounding difficulty

denting his confidence. Bent and bruised
wrapped in determination (an old ploy)

the man tended his crops through
                    uncertain summer

until the avalanche
       made skeletons of cabbages
              flattened the potential for grief
                    honed the spirit in its image.

Ghostly among ghosts
he gathered the stones of his misfortune
placing one upon another to a great height
and stronger than before.

He barred the door; waited for winter.

NO NEED FOR LABELS

I know these pavements by their leaf-prints:
> chestnut round about The Green
> beech mixed with ash along The Lane

and well-remembered puddle-patterns
after rain.
I know the danger of the rising slab
a pot-hole and the taxi-cab
from number six.
No need for name-plates in the fading light.

I know this man by calloused finger-touch
> cooling in summer's heat
> soothing on tender spot

and well-remembered hurt around bright eyes
when life is NOT . . .
I know the danger of a hasty word
the indiscretion overheard
when time plays tricks.
No need for conversation in the night.

It seems as if since world began
I've known these pavements

and this man.

SNOW-BLIND
(A modern Nativity)

Early snow surprised the city
after the intense heat.

I remember the burning
and the scorched eyes
peering from cracks in blackened timber.
We were not ready for such benefice,
such cleansing of the spirit.

Silence arranged itself in small flakes
sifting into crevices
soaking up despair.
Hope skinned over aching wounds
and the people crept out of their hurt.

Then came the refugees . . .
Eden was floor-space in a ruin.

But peace limped through crowded streets
and bitterness burnt holes in Paradise.

I had no cause to complain.
My travellers were a couple set apart,
expecting little
and thanking God for it on the hour.

She was young, nearing her time.
The man, almost a stranger to his youth
bemused, as one caught up in prophecy.

On straw thrown down for cattle
the child was born
and first knew Fortune's prick.

They departed hurriedly, I recall,
looking over their shoulders -
while the town
turned on its side and slept,
unaware of miracles.

CHRYSALIS

Lightning sparks thunder
out there and in my head.

Cocooned in summer duvet -
counting the miles
between the flash and bang -
I pray for double figures
(as old wives dictate)
almost suffocate . . .

Sensing a safe distance
crumpled, limp
I slip from rumpled sheets
into uncanny quiet . . .
fluttering imago.

Splashes of blue
still penetrate
clandestine corners of night
like intermittent fairy lights
out of time and place.

Tomorrow is for trying out wings.

A CAT FROM ALICE

Cats . . . are where
they have no right to be - and that's
not fair! At first, the scene
is peaceful, furless, then
like evanescent Cheshire, purrless -
out of Wonderland - a tail,
tip-rampant as a brigantine in sail -
the next in line a feline claw, a paw
and then another, soon a third
and then its brother, all a law
unto themselves, no path secure
from this triumphant predator.
Remove one's gaze for just a jiff
and there upon the garden shed
the animal complete with head.
What if - I turn again,
would he be gone? Not yet.
We fix each other with the eyes,
mine brown, his yellow.
Determine to outstare the fellow -
concentrate on Pigs and Pepper,
Duchesses and Queens and Kings
and make him slowly disappear
from tipsy tail and paw and ear
to that infuriating grin.

But would the last laugh
be on me . . . or him . . .

STATE CIRCUS IN GROZNY, 1995

There was no advance publicity,
no rush for ringside seats
or dancing in the streets,
no festivity of the usual kind.
A blind man listening for silence
caught the first burst of fire;
felt alien vibrations through mean soles
open to cold and caution
painfully cobbled.
His part was to play Fool, the warm-up fellow
sent on before the main attraction.
Then came gladiators
omnipotent in elephantine tanks;
the chorus marching
well-practised patterns
co-designed off-stage
by generals in padded cells.
High flyers topped the bill,
needed no safety net,
met no opposition.
Dropping lethal cargo
with consummate skill - unasked,
they basked in midnight afterglow.

It was reported later by the press
that some spectators in their eagerness
had strayed too near
and suffered burns. Others froze,

forgot the words -
but ranged in strange
configurations on the ground,
made realistic extras, unsolicited
and unrehearsed. Those cursed
in blackened balcony and pit,
huddled thinly in their hurt, bit
avidly on rotting bread
and prayed for curtain call.

After a long run, diminishing
houses and a changing cast,
the show left town.
Behind, bereft, in ragged line,
like ghoulish clowns, stood
white-faced children
streaked with blood.

HEDGEHOG FLOWER

Ugly it was -
expelled from Wales on a dragon's breath
wrapped in the Western mail
and back-packed to an English town.

Crusty it was -
and barrel-shaped
a dusty ancient (no mere Cyclops)
with a hundred eyes
barbed for close encounters.

Cactus it was -
in hedgehog guise, Echinos (from the Greek)
hiding its instincts
under woolly hats.

Stubborn it was -
sitting unmoved beside begonia-brilliance
until one breakfast in July
beyond the marmalade and streptocarpussies,
the cautious cuttings on the window ledge,
itinerant ivies in the porch,
the greenhouse staging was agog because

growing it was -
a hairy stem, repulsive,
getting longer by the hour -
primeval urge
encapsulated in the bloated tip.
The monster grew . . .
and then at daybreak (unsuspecting)

there it was -
a large white flower:
long slimline petals tinged with pink
too delicate it seemed, to come
from such a curiosity.
Rice-paper water-lily
floating on a lake of air, fading almost
before the paint was dry.

Sudden it was -
and yet how vivid the brief pleasure
of it . . .

THE SLUGGARD

Oh, slug,
oh, ug
ly and unpalatable epithet.
This is no hymn of praise
damp creature
of the darkly brooding night
and dripping days.
Oh, clammy gastropod
moving like Bony's army
on its abdomen -
but not to war,
merely to satisfy
voracious appetite
in secret corners silently
oozing viscidity,
avoiding sun.

Hermaphrodite by strange design
and yet you climb
a mountain wall to find a mate -
make twisted tandem in the round;
from slippery strand suspended,
eat it . . . and
the courtship ended
beat it . . . fall,
all passion vanished,
to the ground.

FIRST OUTING AFTER AN ILLNESS

Today I fried the sun to a frazzle,
popped it onto morning toast
amd bought me a new broom.

Having swept away shadows
(those creeps behind my back)
tied platitudes in plastic bags
and torn "don't" out of the dictionary -
I painted "Hi there!" on my face
and sprinkled me with Joy;

put away the broom,
threw out the crumbs,
sang *Sunnyside Up*,
checked gas taps and smile
and then in style
took tea at Coombe[1].

---

[1]Coombe Abbey restored, refurbished and opened to the public as an hotel,
April 1995.

SPRING CLEAN

She dusted down the days with him,
rejoiced in every feathered flick;
freed shining hours entrapped in glass,
those eager seconds gathered in
the secret corners of her mind
before he left her far behind.

From death's infernal outer space
(forgetting not a single trick)
amœba-like he moved with her,
adjusting to the slowing pace
of age, that curse of all mankind
whose lot it is to stay behind.

Despite detergent, polish, soap,
his presence clung like Evo Stick,
pressed keenly on her new found joy.
Obliterating windowed hope -
despair's impermeable blind . . .
and she a prisoner, behind.

From dreams of Persil-white romance
the answer surfaced, she must pick
another lover - trouble free,
a perfect specimen. Perchance
when next her ex. appeared, he'd find
she was no more bereft, behind.

A moon, illumined by the sun -
she sang the morning, danced a quick
step on the ashes of her past.
Could two be melded into one,
eclipse and, suitably aligned,
at last look forward - not behind?

IMPRESSIONS I - THE BOATING PARTY and BATHERS
(From the paintings of Pierre Renoir and Georges Seurat)

Sunday-free, we took to the boats early -
Gustave and Georges, Aline and the rest,
a weekend crowd in search of fun,
eager to shake off city dust,
surprising a reluctant sun.

Haze hung soft about the river
making ghosts of trees, and then at noon,
as if to please, the day outshone
those peacock-proud with sudden brilliance.
Fingers skimmed water like birds
flirting with reflection; oars splattered
and swished through snatches of laughter
and we closed our eyes and wished . . .

Towards Asnières
we passed a group of workers
from the factory (tall chimneys still in sight) -
their bodies vulnerable and white.
In almost-summer, one young man
stood shivering in shallows, cupped
pale hands across his mouth for warmth.
Another sat Greek-statuesque
upon the bank determined on a tan
while others older and with less to prove
lay sprawled in fuddled thought on grass
undignified but safe, in rumpled
trousers, shirt and bowler hat.

Late afternoon, we roister
in a café bar not far from home.
Beside verandah rail relaxed, replete,
I smile at Gustave telling one more tale
of fish he missed . . . and girls,
and opposite with 'Gyp' her dog - Aline
(I call him Gyp for gypsy, dark and wild) -
she plans to marry our Pierre

who sketches from a corner seat
to catch the moment later
in a rush of brush -
contain us all (before we fade)
on canvas duly stretched and primed
against the loss of memory and time . . .

IMPRESSIONS II - FAMOUS IN THE PARK
(From 'Concert in the Tuileries Gardens', 1862:Édouard Manet)

Don't look now, Mama
but just behind me over there
by the tree is Monsieur Baudelaire,
you know - the poet - quite a beau
it seems, and to my right
that artist fellow, what's-his-name . . .
Édouard, I think, I can't remember who.
We saw his painting recently -
a Spaniard playing a guitar
beside some onions and a jar -
Édouard - I'll get it soon . . . Manet!
Oh, my - what if some member
of the aristocracy comes by.
The Rue de Rivoli, they say
is packed with carriages
all making for this concert in the park.
I must admit the prospect
of a rousing tune by Offenbach,
the latest fashions, smart young men,
is heaven to Parisiennes.

You're not too hot, Mama, I hope?
Oh, no, you brought a fan. That's good.
Poor Fifi is unhappy in the heat.
Perhaps we should have left her with Pierre
at home. She's such a lamb -
I'll pop her on this empty seat.
And what a treat this is for Jacqueline
and Anne. I knew the girls would have some fun.
Good Gracious, Jacquie, now what have you done!
Those spades and buckets were not my idea -
not here. What a mess of sand and water
splashed all over that new dress.
I feel quite faint - the crowd,
the music just a shade too loud. Mama,
that man - Manet - I do believe
he's making sketches of us all.
Oh, dear, my gown - it's not too pale
with this blue bonnet? I almost wore
the lavender - the one with tiny flowers
on it. Then again . . . "Don't be ridiculous,"
Mama replied. "I'm sure
he's far too occupied
to care about your bonnet, Fifi,
and the likes of us. Don't fuss!"

STYLE

If old man devil has to roll his eyes
and strut around, then let him smile,
wear polished shoes and 'draw the broads' in style.

Rather the gangsters wearing trilby hats
and ties with diamond pins - and spats -
who ride about in gleaming chauffeured cars
with painted back seat molls and long cigars

who though renowned for being insincere
at least conceal their sins with a veneer
of charm, benevolence and politesse,
make out their lives akin to godliness.

Today the urban criminal lacks flair,
delights in grunge and stubble, flowing hair
and greasy baseball caps worn back to front;
coarse denim shrunk, distressed - goes off to hunt

on foot or screaming ton-up bike. Afraid
to show his features in a small time raid,
he dons a nylon stocking or a hood
to terrorise old ladies. If you should

be faced one day with an unpleasant task
be bold and, if you must, put on a mask
of joie de vivre, be smart - but all the while
look out for other devils with a smile
and polished shoes . . . and style!

MOT JUSTE

'JUST WINDOWS . . .'
the advert said. But in what sense?
Were *only* windows made
and double glazed and leaded,
stained (or not), securi-locked
and easily maintained,
with usual ten year guarantee,
in brilliant white UPVC
or would this firm produce a door
and as a special offer maybe
even a conservatory?
Do they mean by *just* - a window
fair and square and sitting well
with clear and balanced point of view
exactly right for him or her or you?
A window that *deserves* attention
and a favourable mention.
Is it then a *simple* window
made for *moments* here and now,
disposable, replaced at will
to suit a subtle change of mood,
at one, from frame to sill?

I do believe the ad. has worked
and I'm converted. If I find
that I've been had . . .
am disconcerted by the fact
that JUST WINDOWS are contravening
current Trade Description Acts -
look for yet another meaning
in the Medieval sense . . .
a JOUST, with lances at the ready,
let hostilities commence!

OUT OF TIME
(Lines inspired by Beryl Bainbridge Daily Telegraph April 1995)

Today, she thought, is for the kids who run;
jump stairs by twos and threes. But we who find
our mountains rising year by year, compare
them with the gentle slopes we left behind.

Not keen on Modern Art: the abstract paint
which crawls about the wall in search of its
beginnings; dreary piles of sand and stone -
she asked, "why don't they blow it all to bits?"

And walked straight on to catch her breath beside
a Monet lily pond in summer, sat
(inside her head) beneath a parasol
one Sunday on the Island of Grande Jatte.

Moments to her are stepping stones she treads
each day awash with treachery, and so
on ground which has been tried and still stands firm
she lights a flare against the dark below.

ONE 'FLU' OVER
(The Cuckoo's Nest)

The doctor just had this to say:
bed rest; keep warm, drink something hot.
Bed *nest* is what I feel I've got -
with me, the cuckoo, sitting in it
over-large and puffy-eyed,
quite out of place, an awkward squatter
wrapped in scarves and cardigans;
propped up with cushions, pillows plumped
and snatched from every sleeping space.
Oh, sleep. A word of such serenity and bliss.
To breathe . . . but now the sinuses are blocked
and I am nearer desperation
with each attempt at inhalation.

To pluck from air one measured sniff
does not seem much to ask
but such a task consumes me
through the swollen passages of night.
I swear that if I *were* a bird
I would take flight to some exotic isle
to perch alone and tissue-free
upon a silver singing-tree.

Meanwhile, I wait in tune with grey
for that auspicious day
when I recover taste and smell -
can well believe that for another year at least
this Asian, Chinese, Hong Kong 'flu' is over!

LADY BIRDS
(The 65th anniversary of the Women's League of Health and Beauty at the Albert Hall, 1995)

They came like starlings to a crumb of bread,
those ladies - feathered far more brightly,
bags and costumes all about -
flying Exhibition Road
past Harrods to the Albert Hall.
They came from Manchester and Donegal
from Canada and Aberdeen
and many places inbetween
to celebrate, display
the Health and Beauty exercise
devised by Mary Bagot Stack
for typists in the Thirties, lacking poise.
Incessant bird noise met them in the changing rooms -
wings almost crushed in two foot square,
nerves fluttering - but they were there!

Back home they had rehearsed in draughty barns,
danced weekly in damp halls or paused for breath
in airy palaces with polished floors.

Squeezed into leotards and tights
they limber into stretch and curl,
advance to lunge and twist and whirl.
Oblivious to winter's storm - the farmer's wife
and shop assistant, clerk, the pensioner
leap on, seduced by strains of *Dreams*,
The Way We Were and *Avalon*.
They move around the drip from leaky roof
like ancient dancers round a fire
and like them - imitate, translate
and through such imitation, come to be -
not earthbound clucking hen
but, for a moment now and then
released from domesticity -
a swift in flight, disdainful
of those groundlings far below.

And so it was that festive night -
wings almost crushed in two foot square,
nerves fluttering . . . they were there!

ALL THINGS BRIGHT AND BEAUTIFUL

In 1937 I was nine
and yes - before you ask -
the sun did shine
on all the days that I recall.
And when I garden-wander,
catch a fall of light
I snatch that summer child
and hold her tight.
The world in technicolour hues
sharp focused glows
on classroom walls -
the reds and blues, the greens and golds
of Postman Jim or Grocer Brown,
an engine driver and a clown;
a polished pillar box,
a gleaming train, the pavements
litter free and washed with fairy rain.

Miss Evans, tall and blonde, blue-eyed
returned from teaching in South Africa -
taught us, who never travelled far
beyond the evening star
of our imagination - dreams
played out in lanes between
the houses back to back.
She told us tales
of children who had never seen
the snow - were not white-cold like us

but clothed in dusky skin
burnt umber by the sun,
stayed so as if by magic
which did not rub off.
We modelled huts in plasticine
learned funny words like Kraal
and Hottentot, but did not
comprehend how frail
the living there.
We smelt adventure
and included strangers
in our morning prayers

Today, adventure sleeps
through drought and famine.
Drums beat fear. On screens
too small for life and death
appear no breathless figures
rolled in plasticine controlled
by infant puppeteers
but mothers, fathers,
children old from birth -
fly-ridden bundled bone and dust
on dying earth.

Give us this day our daily bread
and all things bright and beautiful,
they said.

BROKEN THREAD

Stiff with age and cleaning fluid

coat at attention, hooked on habit.
Old man bone-cracking down the morning
limps through another threadbare day
happy-go-button and pocket-free.
Familiarity cradles him
lining his fears against the cold;
snags without hurt rip through thought;
holes know their place and cannot confuse
as he settles deep into the folds of years.

Puffed out with horse-hair platitudes
new-coat-for-old in the dingy hall
hooked on intentions too good for comfort
with too many pockets for money that isn't
so many buttons for fingers that can't -
handsomely tailored but hanging neglected.

Old man sitting alone in his room
weaving together the strands of the past
losing himself in the warp and the weft of it.

NEIGHBOURS

I hear you lonely through the wall
polishing dishes
scraping together the edges of a marriage

allowing fragile memories
to slip
and split
into a thousand images
pricking the senses

sudden recollection
crashes against brass taps -
a swollen door
(there never was the time to mend)
shudders through sadness.

I feel you lonely through the wall
polishing wishes . . .

NEEDLE POINT

Feeling the first invasive chill
of Autumn out of doors,
she went inside
and paused by the embroidery -
her latest effort newly hung,
gilt-edged, secure
behind its non-reflective glass.
She paused, and then moved on
to muse, while supper stewed,
on moments captured, held in place
by needle point and lengths of wool -
the tension right, not pulled too tight
distorting time and space.

Begun on Winter canvas
bare and taut, design took shape
through Summer's slow, beguiling days -
the blaze of flowers near her chair
reflected in the scene she wove.
But seeming harmony conceals a tangled thread -
uncertain starts and careless finishings.

Those bright geraniums were stitched
while men worked loudly overhead
replacing tiles in clouds of dust
and, fittingly, the window box
was sewn in strands of grey and rust
while rotting wood around her home
was, in the jargon of the trade, 'made good'.
Sun baked stone walls
in shades of brown and cream
filled anxious minutes when she sat
on edge, as in a picture frame,
awaiting news - and when it came?
That leaf, there in the corner on the ground,
the one misshapen and alone -
that represents the moment
when she ran towards the phone.

A WELSHMAN'S TALE

He lived halfway up a mountain in south Wales:
halfway between the Miner's Hall
and stars hanging high over Cefn,
the cottages like barnacles
clinging to a ship's bottom.
Down below on a Saturday night
he could hot-foot it to the posh part of Porthcawl
or dawdle in the shadow of Port Talbot steel.
Too young to know the coal beneath his feet,
he knew the sadness of white-faced men
made idle on street corners, blinking in the light,
wanting to be anonymous in dust; cursed
the no-meat days of bread and jam
when his father, Gomer, was a Union man.
And barking down the barefoot years
came old dog Brenin from the farm - and squawks
from geese waylaying him on winter walks -
he never did like geese.
The neighbours called him, "scholarship boy -
the one that went to Bridgend Grammar,
learned to pick up a ball and run . . ."
almost to Cardiff, all aglow in scarlet shirt
and breathing fire with singing ringing in his ears
and passion in his boots.
> But he lost his way (or so they say)
> and came to the Midlands dank and grey
> to study for a Commerce Degree.
> Then on to a post at the G.E.C.
> until the war . . .
> and the Royal Army Ordnance Corps.

What were you doing in the war, Dai?
Building bridges - and building supplies
of guns and paper clips and tanks.
He was good at that, arranging things
with hardly ever a breath between
the thinking and the doing
and he rose to Major from the ranks.
Missed Reveille and Last Post too
when the men were shipped to hell knows where
while he lay in bed with a temperature.

Demobbed in 1947,
no-one expected an instant heaven
but he paid his dues as a Working Man
who remembered days of bread and jam
and the time when money was zipper-tight -
yes, Atlee and Bevan would see them right.

In years of change, he changed direction
to make his mark in education
building bridges and building supplies
of chalk and paper clips and stars.
He was good at that, arranging things
with hardly ever a breath between
the trips abroad and rugger training, student discos,
cricket teams, time-tables and crackpot schemes
passed on to him from hell knows where,
and lesson notes, etceteraire . . !

He climbed some mountains, walked for miles
(avoided geese) and cycled country lanes in peace
unfazed by colleagues' gleaming cars.

As if he were an eager boy,
collecting was his greatest joy.
His books and records and cassettes
filled house and loft and garden shed.
And flower beds were his delight.
He bent his back to weed and hoe
and if he found some earth to spare
he had to plant a seedling there.
He didn't drink and he didn't smoke
yet life was ended at a stroke.

But he never forgot, this lad from Wales,
the no-meat days of bread and jam
and the reasons for being a Union Man.

DEVILS IN THE MORNING

Morning comes too swiftly
after an uneasy night
fragmented by daylight fears;
icicles cut through frosty air.
Out there, beyond this cosy cell
black imaginings played out in dreams
are pavement-hard;
real demons lurk on street corners
eager to break down this fragile shell
and let a thousand torments in.
Better to drift
between blankets of the dark -
escape and a dawn with gentle hands.
But in the meanwhile of our middle years
icicles melt away their little day,
grinning demons whet their claws
and morning comes too swiftly.

A FAREWELL TOO FAR

This Autumn has been going on too long.
Leaves clinging Summer-fast are loath to fall
on pavements damp and inhospitable.
Bewildered birds burst into crazy song
and drag exhausted wings through misty air
as you fly fancies through a fragile mind
in search of yesterday too far behind
to be recaptured from a wheelchair.
One night we felt a sudden, piercing chill,
prepared for Winter but when morning came
the sun shone high. The world was just the same -
the world and you, trapped between seasons still.
Like withered leaves we cling to what we know
though at the turn of year, it's time to go.